BRITAIN IN OLD PHOTOGRAPHS

# THE LONDON BOROUGH OF
# WANDSWORTH

PATRICK LOOBEY

SUTTON PUBLISHING LIMITED

Sutton Publishing Limited
Phoenix Mill · Thrupp · Stroud
Gloucestershire · GL5 2BU

First published 1998

Copyright © Patrick J. Loobey, 1998

Title page photograph: Wandsworth High
Street, c. 1920.

**British Library Cataloguing in Publication Data**
A catalogue record for this book is available from the
British Library.

ISBN 0-7509-1760-1

Typeset in 10/12 Perpetua.
Typesetting and origination by
Sutton Publishing Limited.
Printed in Great Britain by
Ebenezer Baylis, Worcester.

I dedicate this book to the memory of Tony Lee, who was also very interested in the history of Wandsworth.

Patrick Loobey, born in 1947, has lived in Balham, Putney, Southfields and Streatham — all within the Borough of Wandsworth. He joined the Wandsworth Historical Society (founded in 1953) in 1969 and has served on its archaeological, publishing and management committees, being chairman from 1991 to 1994 and also in 1998. Having collected Edwardian postcards and photographs of Wandsworth Borough and surrounding districts for more than twenty-five years, he has a wide-ranging collection (20,000 views plus) encompassing many local roads and subjects. This book complements other recent titles about the Borough of Wandsworth: *Streatham* (1993 and 1996), *Battersea and Clapham* (1994), *Balham and Tooting* (1994), *Putney and Roehampton* (1988 and 1996), *Wandsworth* (1994, 1996 and the present title) and *The Boroughs of Wandsworth and Battersea at War* (1996).

Reproductions of the views in this book are available from Patrick Loobey, 231 Mitcham Lane, Streatham, London, SW16 6PY (Tel. 0181 769 0072).

The captions to the photographs in this book are but a brief glimpse into the varied and complex history of the area. For those seeking further information the Wandsworth Historical Society covers the borough's boundaries, publishing a journal and various papers, the fruits of members' research. Monthly meetings are held on the last Friday of each month at 8 p.m. at the Friends' Meeting House, Wandsworth High Street.

The author must thank and recommend the Local History Library at Lavender Hill, Battersea, where early newspapers, deeds, directories, maps and parish records are made available to those wishing to research names, dates and addresses of families or business concerns.

# CONTENTS

St John's Hill, Clapham Junction, *c.* 1914.

The Lyric Picture Playhouse, Wandsworth High Street, *c*. 1914.

# INTRODUCTION

The photographs within this book cover the five parishes brought together in 1855 to form the District Board of Works and, in 1900, Wandsworth Borough Council. The 1965 reorganization of local authorities resulted in the loss of Clapham and Streatham to Lambeth Council and the amalgamation of the Borough of Battersea with Wandsworth. The areas covered in this book are Battersea, Balham, Tooting, Streatham, Earlsfield, Southfields, Putney, Roehampton and Wandsworth.

The photographs show many of the major changes that have taken place during the twentieth century, including the loss of important buildings owing either to war damage or to redevelopment and also the many parks and small greens donated by benevolent and far-sighted benefactors. The two most prominent words used are demolition and pubs. The breweries have been keen to retain their outlets and the Victorian pubs remain as direction markers in a landscape whose fabric is otherwise being constantly altered by development.

The author would be pleased to hear from people with any memories or comments they wish to share regarding the scenes within these pages.

The Leather Bottle public house, Earlsfield, *c.* 1914.

Garratt Lane, Earlsfield, *c.* 1908.

# WANDSWORTH, SOUTHFIELDS & EARLSFIELD

*Wandsworth Town Hall, corner of the High Street and Fairfield Street, c. 1938. The foundation stone was laid by the Duke of Kent KG, KT on Tuesday, 11 June 1935. The site covered 5 acres and the building was designed by Mr Edward A. Hunt FRIBA and formally opened by Her Majesty Queen Mary on 14 July 1937. The façade facing the High Street has, cut into the stone, an historical tableau of events and industries from the five parishes that make up the borough, namely Wandsworth, Clapham, Putney, Streatham and Balham and Tooting.*

Wandsworth High Street, *c.* 1930. The Wandsworth Palace Cinema on the left was opened on Monday, 13 December 1920 and had a seating capacity of 1,307. The architect was Mr Stanley Beard MSA and it was built by Chinchen & Co. Renamed the Gaumont in 1955, it closed on 4 February 1961 and reopened as a bingo club on 29 July 1961. The bingo club closed and the building was used as a church from 1982 and is now the venue of a night club.

The one structure still intact in this view of Wandsworth High Street from The Spread Eagle public house, on the right, *c.* 1918. The tower of the old town hall, built in 1882 for the parish council, can be seen on the left. The four-storey building in the middle is the old technical college, which was demolished in 1922/3 together with the old shops on the south side of the High Street to make way for the new college opened in 1926.

The post office, 65 High Street, Wandsworth, *c.* 1913. Kohler's shop was also a printer's and stationer's that supplied a range of picture postcards of the local area, much sought after today. J. West, next door, served tea, sandwiches and hot joints between noon and 2 p.m. daily. Further along the road is The Spread Eagle public house.

The junction of the High Street and York Road, *c.* 1920. On the corner is The Ram public house (renamed The Brewery Tap in 1974), which now houses a visitor centre and museum for Young & Co.'s Brewery immediately behind the pub. The Young family bought the brewery in 1831 and, as well as expanding the works, now have control of many public houses in south London and Surrey.

The High Street where the River Wandle is crossed, *c.* 1910. On the left is the distinctive façade of the old Wandsworth baths, opened on 6 July 1901 and demolished in 1968 in preparation for development of the Arndale Shopping Centre. As a result of these alterations, Buckhold Road was diverted and now covers the site of the baths. On the right is The Bull public house, rebuilt in the nineteenth century and destroyed in an enemy air raid on 14 October 1940. The site was left empty and now forms a small park facing the river.

The caption on this photograph from 1912 mentions the River Wandle, but it was an arm of the Wandle called the New Cut which ran in a northerly direction to the west of the main river through what later became King George's Park. The view is from Mapleton Road through the arches of what was locally called the 'Aqueduct', a storm relief sewer that crossed the Wandle valley from Merton Road to St Ann's Hill. The 'Aqueduct' was demolished in 1968.

The tower of the parish church of All Saints in the High Street is most prominent in this view, *c.* 1909. The buildings on the right were drastically altered after the First World War for road widening. On the left is The Old Swan public tavern, seen below in about 1900. To the right is the entrance to the premises of Madge & Lewis, building contractors and also of A.E. Evans, coachbuilder and wheelwright. Sadly these premises were swept away in about 1922/3 for construction of the Ford dealership showrooms and the workshops of Allan Taylor (Motors) Ltd. On 30 March 1882 Mr Wheeles of the Swan, owner driver of a horse bus plying from Wimbledon to the city, drove into the excavations in York Road near Ferrier Street taking place for the South London Tramways. The horse was injured and the bus damaged. He had been operating the service for twenty-six years previously.

The police station, on the left, Wandsworth High Street, opposite Merton Road, *c.* 1912. The station was built in 1883, the same year that the *Wandsworth Boro News*, next door with the blinds out, was founded. Both concerns are still caring for the local community in their own ways.

West Hill, with the police station on the right, *c.* 1910. The only noticeable alteration is the removal of the little railings outside the police station during the Second World War. Behind the trees on the right a little further up West Hill stood the Convent of the Sacred Heart, a teacher training college which opened in 1881. It closed in 1974 when the council bought the site for housing development called The Orchard, named after a large house that stood on the site in the eighteenth century.

The corner of West Hill and Santos Road, *c.* 1910. On the right is the Catholic church of St Thomas of Canterbury, which opened for services in 1895; a tower was added in 1926. On the left is the imposing tower of the London County Council (LCC) fire station, opened on 27 February 1892. The view below is of the station crew fully kitted up for a 'turn out' on their horse-drawn fire engines in about 1908. The leading crewman on each appliance has his whip in hand ready to charge off crying 'Hi, Hi'.

St Thomas' catholic church, West Hill, *c.* 1912. On the far side of Santos Road, to the right of the picture, is West Hill Library, opened in 1885 in the former Putney Lodge, home of the horticulturalist Sigismund Rucker. The library was rebuilt and enlarged in 1937 but retained the Longstaff Reading Room. This was paid for as a gift by George Dixon Longstaff, first chairman of the libraries committee, to commemorate Queen Victoria's jubilee.

West Hill at the junction of Mexfield Road, *c.* 1910. The fire station tower can be seen on the right and behind the trees on the right stands no. 47 West Hill, where Alliot Verdon Roe built his first aircraft in 1906. His company went on to build aircraft such as the Avro 504, the Tutor and the Lancaster. The house was demolished soon after the Second World War and the Longstaff housing estate was built on the site.

Fairfield Street, *c.* 1905. The horse-drawn tram service was started in 1883 by the South London Tramway Co. and ran from Waterloo to Wandsworth, finishing in Fairfield Street at the junction of East Hill and the High Street. In 1906 the LCC electrified the tramway system and diverted the line along York Road alongside Young's Brewery. The track in Fairfield Street was not removed until 1914 and once a year a horse car was brought out to travel the line to extend the council's running rights. The buildings on the right were demolished in the 1920s and '30s for construction of the new town hall.

A horse-drawn bus in Fairfield Street en route to Walham Green, Fulham, *c.* 1906. The horse and cart in the background is travelling along York Road. The LCC renamed many London streets at the turn of the twentieth century: South Street in Wandsworth, between Allfarthing Lane and the High Street, became Garratt Lane and North Street was renamed Fairfield Street.

The Council House, East Hill, *c.* 1908. The building was erected in 1888 for the Wandsworth District Board of Works and taken over by the newly formed borough council in 1900 and used as municipal offices. When the enlarged town hall was opened in 1937 this building was sold to the County of London Electric Supply Co. and renamed County House. From 1953 various finance firms occupied the premises and in 1980 The Book Trust made it their headquarters and called it Book House. East Hill was widened in 1921–2 for extension of the electric tram service and a no. 28 tram en route to Willesden Junction is seen below in about 1930.

Trinity Road shopping parade near Dorlcote Road, *c.* 1907. This section of the street had its own line of six lampposts to light up the shopping establishments.

One young boy delivering a treadle sewing machine takes a rest at the junction of Trinity Road and Burntwood Lane, *c.* 1908. The section of railings on the right penned in the sheep which, until the 1920s, were allowed to graze on Wandsworth Common before being transported to London's markets.

Bellevue Road, *c.* 1908. An early motor delivery van and a furniture removal wagon stand outside The Surrey Tavern public house. The small cast-iron post set into the pavement on the right was an early type of fire alarm – a glass set into the white disc, when broken, would summon the fire brigade.

The parade of shops in Bellevue Road, *c.* 1920. These establishments included at no. 9, Arnold Baldwin, upholsterer, at no. 10, Mrs Margaret Clyma's confectioner's, at no. 11, Miss Venables, draper's, and at no. 12, Cope Bros, provisions. There was also a butcher's, chemist's, dairyman and a confectioner's.

Bellevue Road with The Hope Tavern on the left, on the corner of St James's Road, *c.* 1908. An ice-cream and mineral-water vendor is waiting for some trade from passengers alighting at the nearby Wandsworth Common railway station or from those walking across the adjacent common.

Wounded soldiers rest in the grounds of the Royal Patriotic Asylum, Wandsworth Common, *c.* 1915. Opened in 1857 for orphans of those killed in the Crimean War, the asylum was named in 1914 as the 3rd London General Hospital and held as many as 1,800 patients both inside the building and in tents erected in the grounds. During the Second World War the building was used as an internment camp and interrogation centre for refugees from Europe. The former orphanage and hospital is now used as commercial offices.

Throwing sticks into the ponds on Wandsworth Common for the dogs to fetch is still as popular as it was in this scene, *c.* 1908.

Wandsworth Common railway station viewed from near The Hope Tavern, *c.* 1908. The original station, built in 1856 for the West End and Crystal Palace Railway, stood to the north of Bellevue Road. The London, Brighton & South Coast Railway Co. built the station in its present position in 1869 and rebuilt it in 1894 and 1907.

West Hill, viewed looking towards Wandsworth, *c.* 1908. On the right, two nannies take a rest on a bench with their young charges.

West Hill Road, near the junction of Seymour Road and Wimbledon Park Road, *c.* 1920. The local authority erected a cast-iron railing around the little green in the middle of the crossroads, but this was removed during the scrap drives of the Second World War. Among the trees an earth-covered public air-raid shelter was constructed, which was only removed in the early 1970s and the ground levelled off.

St Ann's church, seen from Rosehill Road, *c.* 1910. The church was designed by Sir Robert Smirke and consecrated on 1 May 1824. Owing to the outline shape of the tower, which can be seen from several miles away, the church is affectionately referred to as the 'Pepper Pot church'.

Killarney Road, off Allfarthing Lane, *c.* 1912. The 1922 directory for Wandsworth lists the following unusual group of surnames for the inhabitants of Killarney Road: Holt, Hill, Wood, Winter, Water, Chappel, Church, Dean, Gold, Pratt, Marshall, Sherrif and Lock.

Aldren Road, leading off Garratt Lane, *c.* 1908. In the background are the premises of the Anglo American Laundry. Having become derelict by the 1980s, the laundry's main block has been renovated and now forms part of housing development.

Garratt Green, with Aboyne Road in the background, *c.* 1906. The lodge to Springfield Farm can be seen on the edge of the green. Prefabricated houses were erected on the green at the end of the Second World War, depriving children of their play area, and were not removed until the 1960s.

The great storm that engulfed south London on 14 June 1914 flooded many streets in Tooting and the River Wandle overflowed and inundated Summerstown, seen here with the old style Surrey wooden clapboard houses still standing. In the eighteenth and early nineteenth centuries the area of Summerstown was a small and compact hamlet which supplied labour for the many mills on the nearby Wandle.

Burntwood Lane, Earlsfield, c. 1908. The trees on the right hide from view Springfield Farm, where cows were still kept until the 1950s. The Springfield Hospital, built at a cost of £63,000 within the grounds of Springfield Farm, was opened on 18 June 1841 with room for 299 patients. Several roads were developed on the left of this view in the 1920s for the Magdalen Park Estate and were named appropriately Openview and Fieldview.

The centre of the little hamlet of Garratt was The Leather Bottle public house, seen here in about 1912. The pub was first mentioned in 1745 but is probably much older. To the left of the pub, in the view below, is the shoeing forge of William Ernest Spiller. The world's first public railway ran in front of this pub between 1801 and 1846. The horse-drawn wagons of the Surrey Iron Railway must have been a common sight as they trundled between Wandsworth and Croydon.

The range of goods available in the shops in Garratt Lane, next to Wilna Road, in 1912 was quite extensive. At no. 305, on the corner, was Gerrard's Pawnbroker's, at no. 303 was George Sutton's tobacconist's and further along the road were a grocer's, a draper's, a butcher's, a dairy and several other stores.

St Andrew's church, Garratt Lane, c. 1907. The church building began in 1889 and the chancel, south chapel and three bays of the nave were consecrated on 8 November 1890. The remainder of the church was consecrated on 1 March 1902, while the clock was added to the wall facing Garratt Lane in 1911 to commemorate King Edward VII.

The staff stand proudly by their display of fruit and vegetables at Edward Bird & Sons' greengrocer's and fruiterer's shop, 461 Garratt Lane, *c.* 1918. The horse and cart was used by Edward Bird's to collect produce from the London markets and nearby farms and to supply their other shop at 557 Garratt Lane. The notice board behind proclaims that properties about to be built on the Magdalen Park Estate could be rented from £42 per annum or the leasehold could be obtained for £530. The picture was probably taken at the corner of Tranmere Road and Magdalen Road.

Garratt Lane with the rail bridge to Earlsfield station in the distance, *c.* 1910. The steam railway first passed through here in 1838 when the London & South Western Railway Co. built the line from Southampton to Nine Elms, Battersea. The station did not open at Earlsfield until 1 April 1884 but then provided a boost to local development.

The Congregational church, Earlsfield Road, *c.* 1912. The board on the front of the building advertises 'Entertainment for the people – every Saturday evening at 8. Admission by ticket one penny.'

An outing for a local club or church group, *c.* 1910. The people are assembled outside the entrance to Charles Henry Cookson's business, 266 Earlsfield Road. Mr Cookson advertised that his was the only dairy farm where the cows were kept on the premises.

Earlsfield Road, *c.* 1910. The road was mainly developed from 1876 onwards by Mr Robert Davies, who had by then acquired 100 acres of land locally. The intention was to build large houses, as seen here on the upper part of the road, but by the time the builders arrived at the lower end of the road, smaller terraced houses was the type of housing people could afford.

Swaffield Road, *c.* 1911. On the left is a notice board for the grandly named Wandle Empire Laundry. The children are either out playing on a Saturday or have just come out of Swaffield Road institution on the right, behind the wall.

Wilna Road, off Garratt Lane, *c.* 1911. Three of the boys are holding iron hoops, the plaything of the time; these were a nuisance in nearby Garratt Lane, where it was often thought a great joke to push the hoop down into the current pick up slot of the tramway and to see the resulting firework display.

Revelstoke Road, Southfields, *c*. 1930. The corner shop was formerly the Wimbledon Park Farm Dairy; in this view it is A.A. Hurworth & Son, butcher's. There is an early style public phone box on the corner.

Sutherland Grove, Southfields, *c*. 1912. The District railway line is to the right behind the fence where in the distance cows are grazing. In 1864 the Royal Hospital & Home for Incurables took over Melrose Hall, West Hill, the former home of the Duke of Sutherland. In the 1930s housing development took place in Sutherland Grove.

Replingham Road, Southfields, *c.* 1912. The Brighton Sanitary Laundry, at no. 138 on the corner of Astonville Street on the left, was the local receiving office for the main works in Alma Road, off East Hill, Wandsworth.

Replingham Road, Southfields, *c.* 1907. A group of young delivery boys chat among themselves while waiting for their next errands from the shops alongside. The far distant skyline is filled with the watch-towers and roofs of Wandsworth Prison on Wandsworth Common.

Southfields railway station, *c.* 1906. The station was built by the London & South Western Railway Co. and opened in 1889. The lower view, from about 1910, is of the Down platform leading to Wimbledon. The interesting thing is the advertisement on the stairs for the Southfields Palace Cinema, on the corner of Standen Road and Merton Road, probably a short-lived enterprise utilizing part of the Baptist church that occupied this corner plot where the Southfields Tyre & Battery Service Ltd now operates from, 288 Merton Road.

Wimbledon Park Road, *c.* 1910. The road surface was still gravel and became a nuisance in hot weather with all the dust kicked up and a quagmire when it rained. To the left of the bushes and group of people is the fence surrounding Wandsworth Technical College playing field, formerly used for sports and the annual Southfields children's flower show. This area would soon be covered with housing.

Coronation Gardens, Southfields, *c.* 1906. To commemorate the coronation of King Edward VII in 1902, the Mayor of Wandsworth, Sir William Lancaster, bought the 2 acres of land and presented it to the people of Southfields as a park. In the background is Merton Road school which was built in 1895; it has been renamed Riversdale School.

Heythorp Street, Southfields, *c.* 1911. Development in this road commenced in 1895 with a few properties erected near the junction with Replingham Road, while the majority of the houses were built in the period 1901–4.

Trentham Street, Southfields, *c.* 1907. Housing development along this road took place mainly in 1905–6 and notices were still outside some of the premises advising that flats were available to let.

Princes' Road, Southfields, *c*. 1907. Until the 1950s this road (renamed Princes' Way) comprised about twenty large houses, whose grounds extended through to Victoria Road (now Victoria Drive). Some of the names of the houses were Oak Lodge, Torwood, Hollywood House, Gordon Dene and Ackcroydon; the latter house gave its name to the council housing estate erected in the 1950s and '60s.

Wimbledon Park Side at the corner of Inner Park Road, *c*. 1906. The small pond is now a little bit overgrown around the edges and the two large houses, with many others on Park Side, have been demolished and replaced with four-storey blocks of council flats.

Merton Road, *c.* 1910. The building with the small turret on the corner of Penwith Road was an off-licence and was converted in 1974 into a Youngs' Brewery public house, named The Pig and Whistle.

The parade of shops in Merton Road, opposite The Park Tavern public house, *c.* 1906. These shops are still an important call for local and passing customers, although the traders do not put their goods on such public display today. Note the young post and telegraph boy on the right standing outside the post office at 197 Merton Road, which is still in operation.

The staff of Bailey & Sons, bakers and pastry cooks, pose with the firm's well-laden delivery carts and wagons outside the premises at 292 Merton Road, on the corner of Standen Road, *c.* 1906. Until the 1940s it was common practice for married women to remain at home and not go out to work. This meant they were able to receive daily deliveries of bread, milk and other perishable groceries.

Brookwood Road, Southfields, *c.* 1907. The modern motorist would probably give his right arm to find so much space on the kerbside.

# CHAPTER TWO

# PUTNEY & ROEHAMPTON

*St Mary's parish church, Putney, c. 1905. The church tower dates from the fifteenth century and the nave was rebuilt in 1836 and remodelled after the 1973 fire. The Victorian shops on the right survived until about 1971, when they were demolished.*

Putney High Street, *c.* 1907. The Great Eastern omnibus is just passing the entrance of the Putney Market, a covered parade of shops that opened in 1904 and eventually closed in the 1930s.

The electric tram service between Putney and Wandsworth was opened in 1911 and the track ran along a short section of Putney High Street between the Thames bridge and Putney Bridge Road. In this view from about 1920, on the left, after the second shop, can be seen the entrance to Putney Market and beyond the Scotch Shoe Stores the façade surmounted with a lamp of the Putney Palace Cinema, which opened in 1913.

Putney High Street, *c.* 1909. Putney Bridge Road is to the right of the motor car. The shop front of J.H. Custance, cigar store, on the right, obscures the roof line, which suggests an eighteenth-century date of origin for the building.

Putney High Street, when all the traffic was horse drawn, *c.* 1880. The building on the left, by the horse and cart, was the original Bull and Star public house on the corner of Lacy Road, rebuilt in 1898 and finally demolished in 1971.

By 1910 Putney High Street had acquired the shops and facilities that are in use today. The large gas lamps on the left are suspended from The Spotted Horse public house. The flag pole on the third entrance on the right is where a small cinema, called the Princes Picture Palace, opened in 1911.

The post office, on the right, on the corner of Disraeli Road and the High Street, *c.* 1930. It opened in 1874 and relocated to the Upper Richmond Road in 1961. Boots the chemists, on the left, occupied this site for approximately seventy years.

Putney railway station, *c*. 1908. The station was first opened in 1846, with the tracks increased to four in 1886 and the present entrance being built in 1902. The three-storey building to the right was demolished in the 1930s and replaced with the five-storey Zeeta House, which opened on 23 February 1938.

The junction of the High Street and the Upper Richmond Road with the Railway Hotel and public house on the left, *c*. 1910. To the left of the bus is the low parapet of the railway bridge, which supports the High Street at this point. The roadway was widened in the 1920s when a parade of single-storey shops was built on the bridge on the left.

The Fulham toll house on Putney Bridge, 1878. Administered by the Fulham Bridge Co., the structure was soon more commonly called Putney bridge. The wooden bridge survived until 1886 when the present stone bridge was opened. The straw-hatted gentleman below is collecting the last toll on the old wooden bridge which was freed of tolls on Saturday, 26 June 1880, the crowd rushing in after the official ceremony and tossing the toll gates into the river.

The Thames sailing barge *Gratitude* being unloaded of bricks destined for local housing development at the draw dock alongside Putney bridge, *c.* 1909. The large block of flats on the left, Kenilworth Court, was built between 1901 and 1903. The other large building, to the left of the river pier, is The Star and Garter public house and mansions, built in 1900.

The embankment at Putney, *c.* 1912. This was constructed in 1886 and before this time the shingle foreshore reached right up to the entrance of the boathouses. The Thames Rowing Club building on the right was built in 1879 and still survives, although the veranda is now enclosed with a glass screen.

The University Boat Race each year is the one time when the town name of Putney becomes famous worldwide. The Putney to Mortlake course has been used since 1845. The Oxford and Cambridge crews are seen preparing for the 1910 race, which Oxford won.

The library in Disraeli Road, *c.* 1906. This building was paid for and given to the people of Putney in 1899 by the magazine publisher George Newnes, who at the time lived at Wildcroft on Putney Heath. Between 1996 and '98 the library was extensively renovated and rebuilt. Between 1980 and '95 it housed the Wandsworth Museum, which was transferred to the Old Court House in Garratt Lane, Wandsworth, in 1996.

Gwendolen Avenue was laid out in 1887, but property building was slow and even by 1894 only two houses had been erected. This view from about 1907 shows the recently completed houses and newly planted trees beyond the junction of Hazlewell Road.

St John's Avenue, *c.* 1908. This road was originally called St John's Road after St John's church, which was opened in 1859. The tower and spire can be seen in the western part of St John's Avenue in this view, which was taken from the eastern part of St John's Avenue. Putney Hill, where the vehicle is passing, divides the avenue in two.

The Jolly Gardeners public house, 61–3 Lacy Road, Putney, *c.* 1906. The little alley to the right is called West Place. The pub was rebuilt in the 1930s.

The Lower Richmond Road, *c.* 1914. Danemere Road is on the left and the advertisement for Ashlone Cycleworks informs us where Ashlone Road is. This scene is still recognizable today except for the addition of a pedestrian crossing where the bus is passing.

The Lower Richmond Road at the junction of Sefton Street on the left and Erpingham Road on the right, *c.* 1914. The three-storey block on the left was demolished in the early 1970s and replaced with a block of flats.

The old adage that directions can be given via pub names is rather apt for Putney and Wandsworth as the area contained many public houses which had been established in Victorian times. In the Lower Richmond Road next to Putney Common is The Spencer Arms on the right and to the left is The Cricketers, seen here in about 1914.

A scramble of young boys crossing Putney Lower Common to return to St Mary's school, to the right, c. 1906. The Spencer Arms public house is in the background. The one shop in the parade was Morrison's Dairy, which kept dairy cows on a farm nearby and supplied milk to many outlets in Putney.

Putney Hill at the junction of the Upper Richmond Road, *c*. 1907. The driver of the horse-drawn bus to Wimbledon is waiting for the trace horse (sometimes called the cock horse), seen coming down the hill beyond the little fountain, to assist in the pull up to The Green Man public house at the top of the hill.

Putney Hill, 1907. This area was occupied by substantial houses that were mostly built in the 1870s but when the ninety-nine-year leases expired in the 1960s the majority of them were pulled down and replaced with blocks of flats.

Tibbets Corner, *c.* 1906. The cameraman was standing on the Kingston Road facing on to West Hill. The imposing gate pillars beyond the signpost lead into Hollywood House. Wimbledon Parkside is to the right beyond the horse trough. In 1969–70 this scene was obliterated with the construction of the four-lane Tibbets Corner underpass.

East Putney station, *c.* 1908. This station on the District railway was built in 1889 to link Wimbledon and the West End. It was actually situated within the Wandsworth parish but it would have sounded clumsy if called West Wandsworth station. The parish boundary marker on the bridge over the Upper Richmond Road, to the right, has been removed.

The Upper Richmond Road with Oxford Road to the left, *c.* 1912. The garden walls to the large houses on the right were all removed in the redevelopments of the 1960s and '80s when poorly designed office blocks were erected here. The Prince of Wales public house, on the corner of Oxford Road, is still pumping out its good cheer.

The Globe Cinema, Upper Richmond Road, *c.* 1920. Opened in 1911 as the Putney Cinema, it survived until December 1976 and was demolished soon afterwards. To the left is The Fox and Hounds public house; a hostelry has stood on this corner since the sixteenth century.

The Wesleyan church on the corner of Gwendolen Avenue was built in 1881–2. The five-storey block of shops and flats on the corner of Charlwood Road, on the left, seen here in about 1928, was totally destroyed by a V1 flying bomb on 18 June 1944. This killed 32 people, seriously injured 23 and slightly injured 62.

The Green Man public house, Putney Heath, *c.* 1898. Judging by the number of people in the scene, it is probably a bank holiday. A pub has stood on this site since at least 1706 and the main structure of the surviving building dates from the eighteenth century.

Grantham House, facing Putney Heath, was built in the 1750s and in 1779–80 became the home of the Archbishop of Canterbury. The house was demolished in the 1930s and in the 1950s part of the Ashburton housing estate was built in the grounds. The small pond on the heath, seen here in about 1898, has since been filled in and small boys can no longer go looking for frogspawn and sticklebacks.

The Telegraph Inn, Putney Heath, *c.* 1908. The pub is named after the Admiralty signalling semaphore station that stood here from 1796 to 1847. The Telegraph road connection with the A3 Kingston road was blocked off with the construction in 1969–70 of the Tibbets Corner underpass and the pub is now situated in a cul de sac.

Putney Park Lane, *c.* 1912. The park was a private hunting ground established in the thirteenth century to supply meat to the manor house at Mortlake. The park reverted to agricultural use in the early seventeenth century and was sold off and split up for villa estates in the eighteenth century.

Expensive horse flesh and motor cars grace the forecourt of The King's Head public house, Roehampton High Street, *c.* 1935. The building probably dates from the 1670s but was used as a pub from the 1720s.

Roehampton when it could still be called a village, *c.* 1907. The Earl Spencer public house on the right is named after the former Lords of the Manor of Wimbledon, which included Putney and Roehampton. The shops on the left were demolished for road widening in 1963.

Roehampton Lane, *c.* 1907. The fountain in front of The Earl Spencer public house was erected in 1882 by the widow of Stephen Lyne Stephens MP, who lived at Grove House, now part of the Froebel Institute situated about half a mile north along Roehampton Lane. In the background is the 200-ft-tall spire of Holy Trinity church, built in 1896–7 to the designs of G.M. Fellows Prynne and opened for worship in 1898.

The High Street, Roehampton, *c.* 1906. The delivery van on the right outside 17 High Street was part of the fleet operated by the bakers W. Glover & Sons, who had several other shops in Barnes and Putney. The firm could supply not only the cakes and food for receptions and parties but also the chairs and tables. Further along the road, on the right, is the sign for The Angel public house.

Medfield Street, Roehampton, *c.* 1912. The group of young girls are standing outside the Hambro Home for Girls, maintained by the Church of England Waifs and Strays Society. The trees in the background were largely removed in the 1950s and the grounds covered by large blocks of flats on the Alton housing estate.

These large houses in Alton Road, Roehampton, seen here in about 1908, were named Strathmore, The Beeches, Mayfield, The Laurels, Heathmere, Dean Lodge, Inverness Lodge, Parkview, Park Lodge, Fernwood and Birchfield. They were built in the 1860s in the grounds of Manresa House. The 1950s saw the introduction of the LCC housing estates and below is part of the Alton estate, seen in about 1955. The circular road sign on the right proclaims the speed limit for motorists is 10 miles per hour.

The National School of Equitation, Roehampton Vale, *c*. 1930. The school, near the Beverley Brook, to the right of the picture, provided tuition in riding, jumping and how to play polo.

The Bald Faced Stag public house, Putney Vale, *c*. 1935. This eighteenth-century pub was the haunt of the highwayman Jerry Abershaw, who was caught and hanged at Kennington in 1795. The pub premises was more famously known as the factory of KLG sparkplugs, started in 1912 by the racing driver Kenelm Lee Guinness. When the factory was rebuilt in 1937 the former pub was demolished. The whole site was cleared in 1989 and an Asda supermarket erected. Stag Lane, by the motor car to the right, leads to the Putney Vale housing estate, which was built in the 1950s.

# CHAPTER THREE

# BATTERSEA

*St Mary's parish church, Battersea, c. 1910. Despite a possible mention of a church at Battersea in a charter dated AD 1067, the earliest reliable evidence of a church here is in a charter dated AD 1157 which refers to a chapel at Wandsworth and a church at Battersea. The present church dates from 1777. There are monuments to Lord Grandison, Viscount and Lady Bolingbroke and many others here. The church was used in a wedding scene for the 1966 film* Alfie, *which starred Michael Caine, Shirley Anne Field and Denholm Elliot.*

St John's College and Battersea House, Vicarage Crescent, photographed from the West London Extension Railway Co. bridge, *c.* 1906. The land for Vicarage Gardens, seen below in about 1910, was bought by the Battersea Vestry with the aid of a £1,000 donation, and opened to the public on 9 May 1896. The Rank flour mills, seen on the far right, below, were demolished in 1997–8 and a large block of luxury flats will soon be completed on the site.

St John's Hill, Battersea, c. 1928. The area is commonly called Clapham Junction but that name is really only relevant to the nearby misnamed railway station. Arding & Hobb's department store towers above everything else in the background. The Imperial Cinema, later renamed The Ruby, and the Barclay's Bank next door were demolished in the 1980s.

This view of Arding & Hobb's department store was taken only a few months before the disastrous fire on 20 December 1909 which destroyed the whole building and killed eight people. The new store, seen in the photograph above, was opened for business on 5 December 1910. The policeman in the road was on point duty. The point where he stood had to be manned for eighteen hours each day, several people fulfilling the duty of directing traffic, giving assistance and making the public aware of their presence.

The three buildings on the right have all been replaced since this photograph was taken in about 1930. The post office, beyond the street lamp on the right, was rebuilt in 1961. Battersea Borough Council supplied electricity to local consumers from a power station in Lombard Road, near the Thames, and built the white-stone showrooms with the clock, on the right, called Electric House. Electric cooking demonstrations were held here twice a week; the building has now been replaced. Beyond the tram is the Pavilion Cinema, which opened in 1916 and was destroyed on 17 August 1944 by a V1 flying bomb, causing twenty-eight casualties. A supermarket was built on the site in the 1980s.

Lavender Hill, *c.* 1928. The library, on the right, was opened on 26 March 1890 by Mr A.J. Mundella MP. The post office, on the left, was opened in 1898 and rebuilt in 1961.

The Shakespeare Theatre, on the corner of Lavender Hill and Theatre Street, was opened in 1896 for dramatic productions and converted for cinema performances in 1923. Badly damaged by fire bombs in 1940, it was demolished in 1957. On the next corner, the building with the balustrade is Battersea Town Hall, opened in 1893. Since the amalgamation of Wandsworth and Battersea Boroughs in 1965, the building has found a new lease of life as the Battersea Arts Centre.

Lavender Hill, c. 1910. A notice on the front of the small dairy cart proclaims the firm's slogan 'Purity – Punctuality – Cleanliness'. The roof of the Ascension church, completed in 1893, can be seen on the left.

Lavender Hill, near the corner of Taybridge Road, *c.* 1910. An oil store on the right has a wonderful display of tin baths, buckets and household utensils outside the premises.

A no. 26 tram passes by the demolished premises of A.B. Hemmings baker's on the corner of Cedars Road and Lavender Hill, August 1950. The brakes had failed on a no. 34 tram descending Cedars Road on 23 August and it had jumped the tracks smashing into the baker's shop. The tram driver was trapped in the wrecked car and two passengers were injured. The shop was rebuilt and today looks as it did before the accident. In July 1946 a tram sped clean across the junction into Queenstown Road and crashed on to its side, shattering the upper deck.

Almost 2 miles from Clapham and entirely in Battersea is Clapham Junction railway station. The high level entrance on St John's Hill had been rebuilt and enlarged by the London, Brighton & South Coast Railway in 1910 when this photograph was taken.

The Surrey Hounds public house, on the left, on the corner of Plough Terrace and St John's Hill, *c.* 1912. This pub was destroyed by a V1 flying bomb on 17 June 1944. St John was the family name of the Lords of the Manor of Battersea, who held the title from 1627 to 1763 when the Spencers of Althorp, Northampton gained the estate.

Arding & Hobbs' department store overshadows the other shops in the shopping district of St John's Road, *c.* 1912. Before 1865 the Falcon brook flowed along here through a series of cascades.

Falcon Road, *c.* 1928. A falcon was chosen for the crest of the St John family and this was recalled in the naming of the road. The large building in the background on the corner of York Road is The Prince's Head public house; the pub name was given on bus and tram routes. The pub was demolished in 1977 for a road-widening scheme.

Northcote Road, *c*. 1912. The road was once famous for the number of market stalls and the variety of produce available. The tower of the Baptist church, completed in 1889, can be seen on the right.

Albert Bridge Road, *c*. 1910. Albany Mansions is on the left and further along the road is the church of St Mary le Park, opened in 1883 and since demolished. In the distance is the Albert bridge, dating from 1873.

The hoarding on the wall in Battersea Bridge Road, beyond the motor car, is advertising the latest Charlie Chaplin film, *The Pilgrim*, made in 1923. St Stephen's church is on the right-hand corner.

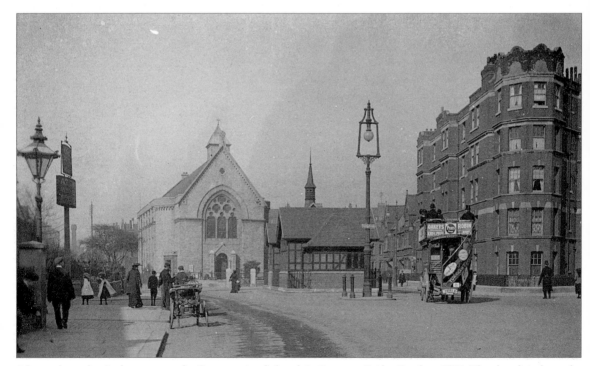

A horse-drawn bus is about to pass the Congregational church in Battersea Bridge Road, *c.* 1906. The church is due to be demolished in 1998 and will probably be replaced with a block of flats. Cambridge Road is to the right of the bus, en route to Kensington Church Street. Surrey Lane is to the left of the church.

The junction of Battersea Bridge Road and Westbridge Road, *c.* 1910. On the left is The Prodigal's Return public house and further along the road on the right is The Earl Spencer public house. There are four 'Spencer' pubs in the borough of Wandsworth and this is the third to appear in this book.

Battersea bridge, *c.* 1912. The bridge was designed by Sir Joseph and Mr Edward Bazalgette and opened on 21 July 1890. The LCC fire station beside the bridge was one of four in London that housed the teams which operated the London Fire Brigade firefloats.

Battersea Park Road, *c.* 1912. The Prince's Head public house, on the corner of Falcon Road, is the dominant building. In 1909 a Captain Windham of the Windham Detachable Motor Body Works, 20A–26A St John's Hill, Battersea, had an aeroplane constructed of bamboo assembled on the roof of the pub, but when it was tried at Wembley it was unsuccessful.

Christchurch, Battersea Park Road, *c.* 1912. The church was dedicated on 27 July 1849 but was wrecked on Sunday, 21 November 1944 by a direct hit from a V2 rocket which brought the tower and spire crashing down and also killed the vicar's mother. A smaller church was built on the site after the war.

Battersea Park Road, with Albert Bridge Road on the left and The Clockhouse public house on the right, *c*. 1912. All of the buildings on the right, beyond the pub, were demolished in the 1960s for local authority housing development.

Battersea Polytechnic in Battersea Park Road opened in 1894 and many of Britain's engineers and scientists have been trained there, among them Sir Alec Issigonis, designer of two famous models of cars, the Morris Minor and the 1959 Mini. The student roll in the 1940s exceeded 8,000, including day and evening attendance.

Battersea Rise, *c.* 1910. The individual stores on the Rise are slowly disappearing as more restaurants have been opened during the 1980s and '90s.

Until 1858, when the British Land Co. started development, Bolingbroke Grove was formerly called Five Houses Lane, the number of properties in the road at that time. The road is named after a descendant of the Lord of the Manor, Sir Oliver St John, Viscount Grandison, who became Viscount Bolingbroke in 1712.

Bolingbroke Hospital, Bolingbroke Grove, shortly after the major rebuilding programme of the early 1930s. In 1880, when opened, the hospital occupied Bolingbroke House, one of the five houses in the road, then known as Five Houses Road. Below, in about 1930, is the Annie Carmichael ward for children at the Bolingbroke Hospital.

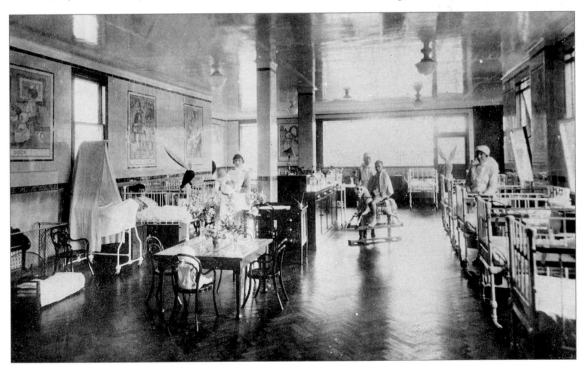

A horse-drawn bus struggles up Broomwood Road, *c.* 1907. William Wilberforce, who was the driving force behind the emancipation of slaves in 1833, lived at Broomfield, a large house that stood behind what is now 111 Broomwood Road.

Chatham Road, *c.* 1907. The valley cut-through by the Falcon Brook is very discernible, with Northcote Road at the lower end and the other half of Chatham Road rising in the distance to meet Webb's Road.

Several delivery vehicles and delivery boys going about their tasks in Barnard Road, *c.* 1907. The view is from Lavender Sweep with St John's Road at the far end.

Belleville Road, *c.* 1910. In the distance, on the corner of Webb's Road, is Belleville Road school with its distinctive bell tower. Northcote Road divides Belleville Road in two at the point where the two ladies are standing.

Grandison Road, *c.* 1910. The St John family had as part of their name the title Viscount Grandison, which can be traced back to 1335 when William de Grandison died, a descendant of Lady Margaret Beauchamp who married Oliver St John in the fifteenth century.

The development of Mallinson Road was approved in 1869 by Battersea Vestry, the local authority at the time. On the right is the Baptist chapel, opened on 9 July 1887.

# CHAPTER FOUR

# BALHAM

*Balham High Road viewed from Upper Tooting Road, c. 1928. The old Methodist chapel, on the right, was replaced by St Anselm's Catholic church in 1933. Repairs to the road surface on the right were being undertaken by the Improved Wood Pavement Co. Ltd.*

The parade of shops between Louiseville Road and Drakefield Road on Balham High Road, *c.* 1912. The street lamps seem small in comparison with the tall modern lighting systems but were thought adequate for assisting pedestrian traffic.

Balham High Road, near Ritherdon Road, *c.* 1910. The trees conceal the large private houses built in the 1850s and '60s. These gardens were soon to be covered over with shops or, as on the left, the 1930s block of flats called Ducane Court.

Several trams have been halted owing to a wheel coming off a coal merchant's cart, *c.* 1906. The photograph was taken from the American camera studios at 259 Balham High Road. The passengers on the tram have the best view of all the chaos while many pedestrians gather around. The scene below shows a police constable taking details from the tramway staff after the cart has been moved aside and the bags of coal have been stacked against the kerb.

Ducane Court, Balham High Road, *c*. 1938. This eight-storey building contained 647 apartments, the largest block of flats under one roof in Europe; building began in the mid-1930s and was completed in 1936. One of the services provided was a wireless announcement system in each flat.

Balham High Road, *c*. 1914. The row of shops on the right was called Station Parade and was built in 1904. On the corner of Oakmead Road, on the right beyond the parade of shops, is the Balham Palladium Cinema, which was opened in 1914 but was destroyed by bombing during the Second World War.

The west entrance to Balham Underground station soon after opening in 1926. The similarity in design of this station and Clapham South (see p. 88) and the other stations on the Northern Line of the Underground system is quite noticeable – they were all designed by Charles Holden. The line from Clapham High Street was opened on 13 September 1926 but owing to an industrial dispute Balham station was not opened until 13 December 1926.

An unseen policeman has halted the traffic on Balham High Road at the corner of Station Road, *c.* 1913. Tram route numbering was only introduced in 1913. The detail in this scene is remarkable: a young boy on the right with an iron hoop, a Boy Scout troop waiting to cross the road, a young man attempting to restart his early motorcycle, a flower seller on the pavement by the bank, the enamel clover-leaf tramstop on the left, the no. 61 bus en route to Richmond and four electric trams, two are almost hidden by the nos 2 and 6 trams.

The older houses in Balham High Road, dating from the 1850s, had single-storey shops built on the front gardens in the late Victorian period, as seen here in the shopping parade near the station, *c*. 1914. The sandwich-board man on the right is advertising margarine and tea available at the Maypole Dairy Co. premises at 27 High Road, Balham.

Two ornate buildings on Balham High Road that no longer exist are seen on the left. The first is the South Metropolitan Gas Co. showroom and the other is the Pyke's Circuit Cinematograph, built in 1911 and renamed on many occasions, becoming the Rex, the Picture House and the Ritz. Asian films were shown here in the few years before demolition in 1985.

Balham High Road, *c*. 1930. Hildreth Street and market is to the right. Ramsden Road is to the left of the street lamp.

Holdron's department store occupied several shop frontages on Balham High Road on either side of Balham Grove, as seen here, *c*. 1912. The shops were demolished and have now been replaced by a supermarket, set back from the High Road.

Cornell's butchers, to the right on the corner of Old Devonshire Road and Balham High Road, had a decorated cast-iron canopy in front of the shop which was subsequently removed. Further along the road on the corner of Balham New Road is The Duke of Devonshire public house, which was advertising the 'Finest three course luncheon' for 1*s* 6*d* when this photograph was taken in 1926.

The Balham Assembly Rooms, 38 Balham High Road, on the corner of Lochinvar Road, *c.* 1910. The building was used for many social functions and was the local centre for the Salvation Army, but was badly damaged by a flying bomb in 1944 and rebuilt in 1957.

The Balham Hippodrome, on the corner of Balham Hill and Yukon Road, *c.* 1910. Opened on 18 September 1889 as the Royal Duchess Palace, the theatre cost £35,000 to build and was later renamed the Balham Hippodrome. Popular acts of the time such as Sophie Tucker and Billie Williams would appear before an audience of 2,500. The building was badly damaged by bombing during the Second World War and demolished, the site covered by a block of council flats.

The George Hotel, Balham Hill, *c.* 1918. The pub was first established on the other side of the road in 1715 and resited in 1778 to the present location. It was rebuilt in 1888 with facilities provided alongside by H. Baker Ltd to cater for the stabling and hiring of horses, wedding carriages and taxis.

Balham Hill, *c.* 1913. The row of shops near Hazelbourne Road have all the blinds down to protect the goods on display from the sunlight. On the left are some large trees in the gardens of houses demolished in the early 1920s for the extension of the Underground railway, see below.

The original intention was to call this station Nightingale Lane, after the road on the right, but when it opened on 13 September 1926 the name unveiled was Clapham South station. Balham North would have been more accurate and Nightingale Lane more acceptable. The stations on the route to Morden were designed by Charles Holden, as was the circle and bar logo of the Underground system. In 1937 a five-storey block of flats called Westbury Court was built above the station and shops.

The junction of Balham High Road with Bedford Hill, *c.* 1906. The street traders, or costermongers, were moved to nearby Hildreth Street, where the market still thrives.

What must have been the smallest cinema in Wandsworth is seen here on Bedford Hill, *c.* 1912. In 1911 the shop on the left, on the corner of Shipka Road, was converted into the Bedford Hill Cinema with 100 seats costing only 1*d*; reserved seating cost 2*d*. In 1914 a series of safety acts were brought in regarding number of exits and fire regulations and this resulted in the closure of these small cinemas and, at the same time, the opening of larger premises such as the Balham Palladium in the High Road.

The Bedford Hotel and public house, Bedford Hill, *c.* 1908. Here in 1876 the inquest took place into the mysterious death by poisoning of Charles Bravo, who lived at The Priory, 225 Bedford Hill. Whether the culprit was his wife Florence, who had been having an affair with the family doctor, or another member of the household is still unknown.

Bedford Hill, from Tooting Bec Common, *c.* 1912. The first house on the right was called Culverdon and was built in the late 1880s.

One of the shortest roads in Balham, Beira Road, was photographed in 1912 by Mr R.J. Johns of Longley Road, Tooting. Mr Johns left a record of his work in the form of the picture postcards he published between 1911 and 1936. (See page 117.)

Byrne Road, Balham, *c.* 1920.

Cavendish Road, Balham and Clapham, *c.* 1910. Cavendish House, demolished in 1905, was the home and laboratory of the eminent chemist Henry Cavendish. It stood on the corner of Dragmire Lane, which was later renamed Cavendish Road to commemorate the famous scientist who calculated the weight of the Earth. Englewood Road is on the right.

A dog is asleep in the doorway of the Cavendish Dairy, on the corner of Dagnan Road, Balham, *c.* 1920. Before the 1950s and the introduction of supermarkets and mechanized delivery of milk to the doorstep there were many of these small dairies supplying local districts.

Elmbourne Road, Balham, with Tooting Bec Common on the right, *c.* 1910. The road is named after a small stream, the Elmbourne, that ran across the common nearby.

Emmanuel Road, *c.* 1926. The road name stems from the purchase in 1629 of nearby Hyde Farm by Emmanuel College, Cambridge. The farm house stood where 46–56 Emmanuel Road were built.

Hazelbourne Road, Balham, *c.* 1906. Hazelbourne was the name of a large house, facing Balham High Road, demolished to make way for development of this road when it was laid out in 1878, then known as Westlands Road. The turning on the left beyond the group of girls is Westlands Terrace.

A winter's day with a horse 'taking on fuel' at the trough on the corner of Nightingale Lane and Bolingbroke Grove, 1909. The crossroads seen here have been altered in layout since this photograph was taken, but the curve of the tree line on the left can still be seen on this corner of Wandsworth Common where Bellevue Road meets Bolingbroke Grove.

Nightingale Lane, c. 1906. Previously it had been called Balham Lane and Balham Wood Lane. It was developed in the 1860s with large houses on the former Old Park Estate. The tower on the right is part of Nightingale House, erected in 1871 to the designs of R. Richardson. As a nursing and residential complex, it now houses 400 residents as the Home for Aged Jews.

Nightingale Lane, c. 1910. The lane is a very old route that linked Wandsworth and Clapham commons and is said to have acquired its name from nightingales that sang in the tree-lined lane before development took place.

Balham Public Library, Ramsden Road, *c.* 1906. The library was opened on 3 June 1898 and built on land donated by Sir Henry Tate, the sugar magnate. The building was remodelled and enlarged in 1988–9 and reopened on 12 January 1990.

Ramsden Road, *c.* 1913. Although the road was laid out by the early 1860s, housing construction only began in 1876. It is evident that development here was piecemeal with various designs of properties erected by individual developers in the nineteenth century.

Ravenslea Road, Balham, *c*. 1920. In the far distance can be seen the two chimneys on the roof of the Balham Hotel public house which lies on the corner of Boundaries Road and Chestnut Grove.

St James's Drive, Balham, *c*. 1910. Children gather outside the four small shops that once stood on the corner of Sarsfield Road. The street at this time was called St James's Road and, strictly speaking, lies in Battersea and not Balham. In 1917, when designating London postal codes, the General Post Office did not adhere to parish boundaries and allocated them for their own convenience.

Thurleigh Road with Montholme Road on the right, *c.* 1908. Wandsworth Common is in the far distance. The hand-pushed cart on the left was for delivering Mann, Crossman & Paulin's stouts and ales.

St Luke's church in Thurleigh Road, *c.* 1910. The church was built in 1883–9 to the designs of F.W. Hunt. The tall square bell tower, surmounted by a golden cross, was added in 1892.

Upper Tooting Park, Balham, *c.* 1920.

Yukon Road, Balham, *c.* 1914.

Lister & Co. tea merchants and blenders,
19 Bedford Hill, *c.* 1908. The store also stocked
wines and spirits. The gas lamp certainly
advertised the whereabouts of these premises.
With the advent of supermarkets and their one-
stop shopping facilities it has proved difficult for
specialist shops such as this tea merchants to
survive.

The premises of C.J. Quinn, jewellers, at 64 Balham
High Road, *c.* 1914. Jewellery and umbrella repairs
were carried out on site. The window display is
mainly of clocks and watches in a variety of sizes and
materials, but also includes jewellery and cutlery.

# CHAPTER FIVE

# TOOTING & STREATHAM

*The tram terminus at Tooting Junction railway station, 1913. This is where the LCC tramway system met the South Metropolitan Tramway from Croydon and passengers wanting to continue their journey had to transfer on to the other system. On the left is the aptly named Railway Bell public house.*

Amen Corner, Tooting, *c.* 1913. The name probably derives from the ancient ceremony of beating the bounds of the parish which would end with a prayer and the accompanying party finishing events with a loud 'Amen'. Knapton's ironmonger's stores on the corner has every inch of space taken up with a display of tin baths, buckets, sprinklers and a host of other items.

Carriages line up in Mitcham Road, near Bickerstaff Road, for The Old Mitre outing, 16 August 1914. The Old Mitre public house is to the right. The banner above the third carriage has the slogan 'Blokes 4 Women'. Britain had been at war with Germany for twelve days when this outing took place.

The Tooting Electric Pavilion Cinema, Mitcham Road, with workmen putting the final touches to the building before opening in 1914. The cinema frontage was remodelled and by 1946 it was called the Astoria. The last film was shown on 11 April 1970 and the building demolished shortly afterwards. Next door is The Mitre public house, an old coaching stop, which was rebuilt in 1906.

Mitcham Road, Tooting, c. 1926. On the left is The Foresters' Arms public house, recently renamed Jack Beard's after a publican of that name.

The Granada Cinema, Mitcham Road, Tooting, probably photographed during the week it opened; behind the caption, workmen's ladders have been laid across the entrance steps . The 4,000 seat cinema, designed by M. Komisarjevski was opened on 7 September 1931. The last film shown was *The Good, The Bad And The Ugly* on 17 November 1973 and the building was converted into a bingo hall in 1976 and is now called the Gala. The interior decoration is considered a masterpiece of cinema architecture and the cinema is now a listed building.

Mitcham Road, Tooting, *c.* 1926. The Methodist Central Hall looms over the other buildings. The hall was opened on 10 November 1910 and was mainly funded by a donation of £14,000 from Joseph Rank, owner of many flour mills, who lived at the top of Church Lane, Tooting. The main hall could seat 1,800 and cinema shows were given, but it was demolished in 1967 and a Marks and Spencers store built on the site.

This stretch of Mitcham Road is commonly termed Tooting Broadway, although that name does not appear officially anywhere, except on the Underground railway station. The Temperance Billiard Hall, on the right, was demolished in the early 1920s to make way for the construction of Tooting Broadway station.

Tooting Broadway station, on the left, *c.* 1927. The station was opened on 13 September 1926. Behind the bus are the Tooting indoor swimming baths, opened in 1907 by the Mayor of Wandsworth, Councillor James Wise. The baths cost £6,000 to build and were closed in 1977 and demolished in 1981. The statue of King Edward VII was unveiled on 4 November 1911 by Councillor Archibald Dawney, Mayor of Wandsworth. The roadway and pavement were altered in 1994 and the statue was moved nearer to the station. Shortly after the move, the sword was stolen from the statue.

Eastbourne Road and Seely Road, Tooting after the great storm, Sunday, 14 June 1914. The crowd are standing on the bridge over the River Graveney, which had burst its banks. In the distance are the grounds of Furzedown House, soon to be covered with housing.

Tooting High Street from the rail bridge, *c.* 1910. This spot was the terminus for the LCC tramway system and where the London United Tramway Co. trams terminated. The LUT trams were operated from an overhead current pick-up or trolley and the LCC trams had the conduit slot current collection system. Although the LCC trams were introduced here on 13 October 1907, a physical connection to allow through running was only made in 1922.

A no. 32 bus travelling along Tooting High Street is about to pass Hoyle Road, *c.* 1930. The noticeable difference in this photograph to others in the book is the number of private automobiles on the roadway and the lack of horse-drawn traffic.

When the electric tram service was introduced in 1903 the terminus was near Totterdown Street. The line was extended as far as Tooting High Street near Garratt Terrace in 1905. The trams are waiting at the terminus, either in 1905 or 1906. Defoe Road, on the right, was later renamed Garratt Lane. To the left of the tram are the premises of the auctioneers and estate agents, James Fisher, demolished for construction of the Underground station.

A horse-drawn removal van from J. Carpenters, 69 & 71 Bickersteth Road, Tooting, is turning out of the High Street into Mitcham Road, viewed from Garratt Lane, 1907. A few of the older village buildings are seen in the background, but they would survive only for another year or two.

A policeman on point duty has his work cut out as trams and buses gather at the crossroads of Garratt Lane, Mitcham Road and High Street, Tooting, *c.* 1914.

Tooting High Street, near the Garratt Lane corner, *c.* 1914. Some small eighteenth-century buildings on the left had survived but did not do so for much longer, soon to be replaced by larger shops.

David Greig's grocery shop at 1 & 2 Upper Tooting Road, is well hidden from the sunlight with the blinds out, *c.* 1914. In wet weather it was possible to walk for several hundred yards under the shop awnings without getting wet.

The Mayfair Cinema, Upper Tooting Road, was opened on 15 February 1932, with a seating capacity of 1,839. Renamed the ABC Cinema, but later reverting to the name Mayfair, it closed on 13 January 1979 and was converted into a bank. The photograph was issued to advertise the cinema when it was new.

Upper Tooting Road, *c.* 1928. The Central Hall Cinema, on the left, was opened on 14 October 1910 and was later renamed the Classic Cinema; it finally closed on 21 March 1983. The building survives as a private club and retains the name Classic.

This scene was taken about two years after Trinity Road Underground railway station was opened on 13 September 1926. The station was renamed Tooting Bec in 1950. Upper Tooting Road is to the right and Balham High Road is on the left.

Avarn Road, Tooting, *c.* 1914. In the background, in Mitcham Road, is St Boniface Roman Catholic church. Built in 1907, the church was adorned in 1927 with a bell tower and a Byzantine front elevation.

St Nicholas' parish church, Tooting Graveney (the correct name of the town), viewed from Bickersteth Road, *c.* 1905. The church was opened in 1833 and the earlier church, probably dating from Saxon times, was demolished soon afterwards. The small eighteenth-century cottages on the left corner were to last only a few more years, the old Surrey village charm being lost to London's urban sprawl.

The Grove Hospital, Tooting Grove, *c.* 1914. The Grove Hospital for Infectious Diseases was opened on 17 August 1899 and during the First World War was used as an isolation hospital for wounded troops. The hospital was renamed St George's in 1954 and has been enlarged considerably since the London St George's hospital and medical school transferred here in 1980.

The turret of the Methodist Central Hall in Mitcham Road, Tooting, can be seen in the distance in this photograph taken from Blakenham Street, Tooting, *c.* 1914.

Brenda Road, Tooting, *c.* 1912. This road had the unwelcome distinction of being bombed during the First World War. Six people were killed here in an air raid in 1917 and also at Romberg Road, Tooting; among the victims was a Mr Page and his son, a bugler with the scouts who was to have sounded the 'All clear'.

Church Lane, Tooting, 1911. To the right is the Tooting Home, built in 1888 as St Joseph's Catholic College. In 1895 it became a home for the aged poor and was taken over in 1914 for use as a military hospital. In 1923 it became St Benedict's Hospital. The building was demolished in 1985 but the fine clock tower and entrance columns were re-erected in the middle of the housing estate constructed on the site.

St Benedict's Hospital and Church Lane, photographed from the tower of St Nicholas' parish church, *c.* 1925. The wooden huts on the left of the field were erected by the YMCA during the First World War as recreation rooms for wounded troops being treated at the hospital.

Church Lane, *c.* 1911. The parish church stands at the bottom of the tree-lined lane, which has an air of rural tranquillity.

Franciscan Road, Tooting, *c.* 1906. This road was known as Ensham Street at this time. Dewey Street is to the right by the milkman pushing his dairy cart.

Franciscan Road school when it was still called Ensham Street school, *c.* 1906. The school is now an adult education centre.

Children gather outside the tobacconist's and newsagent's shop of E. Aslett on the corner of Garratt Lane and Bellew Street, Tooting, *c.* 1912. They are probably mainly interested in the range of confectionary and mineral waters on sale there.

Longley Road, Tooting, *c.* 1911. The motor car is standing outside the premises of the photographer Mr R.J. Johns at no. 171; his output of London suburban scenes amounts to over 12,000 and he photographed virtually every Tooting and Balham street.

Loubet Street, Tooting, *c*. 1911. The street is probably named after Emile Loubet who was voted on to the French national assembly in 1876, filled the office of Premier in 1892, was President of the Senate in 1895 and from 1899 to 1906 was the President of France.

Mandrake Road, *c*. 1911. In the far distance in Topsham Road are some green fields, soon to be covered over with bricks and mortar.

Development of Rectory Lane took place between 1908 and 1912 and was almost complete by the time this photograph was taken. The old hedgerow was removed and a pavement laid. The former name, Back Lane, dating back to medieval times, was also changed.

Sellincourt Road was developed by Messrs Swain & Seely at the beginning of the twentieth century. Sellincourt Road school was built by the LCC in 1907 and, although badly damaged on 6 March 1945 by a V2 rocket which fell in nearby Nutwell Street, the school is still in use.

Newlands House, Tooting Bec Road, alongside the common, was first mentioned in 1847 and until 1881 was a private household. By 1891 an institution called the Asylum for Gentlemen of Unsound Mind had occupied the house. They remained there until 1939 and the house was demolished in about 1950 to make way for council housing.

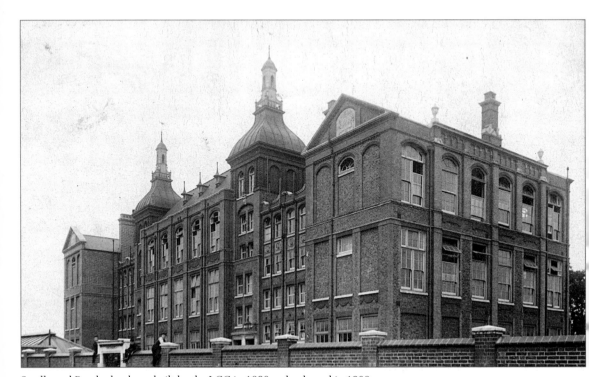

Smallwood Road school was built by the LCC in 1898 and enlarged in 1908.

The shops in Mitcham Lane, Streatham, between Aldrington and Thrale Roads, were built on the front gardens of the houses, as seen here, *c.* 1910. Following the reorganization of the London Boroughs in 1965, approximately 75 per cent of Streatham passed to the London Borough of Lambeth, with the rest remaining in the London Borough of Wandsworth. Mitcham Lane, south of the railway line to Streatham Common, remains in Wandsworth.

Children pose for the photographer Mr R.J. Johns in the middle of Mitcham Lane, 1912. On the corner of Welham Road are two churches, the Baptist church, erected in 1902 and which had its spire removed in the 1960s, and St James' church, which was completed in 1914.

A tram has just negotiated the notorious curve at the corner of Southcroft Road and Mitcham Lane, *c.* 1910. A few trams turning into Southcroft Road had previously run off the rails and in 1913 a tram turned over, badly injuring the conductor.

The shops in Thrale Road, Streatham, *c.* 1920. The road was named after Mrs Thrale, who in the eighteenth century entertained many members of society, including the lexicographer Dr Samuel Johnson, at Streatham Park. Many wealthy residents lived in the substantial properties in this road, among them Mr Charles Derry, of the well-known department store Derry & Toms.

The newly opened shops in Moyser Road, Streatham, *c.* 1908. The first three outlets are let and the fourth was, according to the board above the entrance, about to be taken up by the Don Tailoring Co., which promised ladies' and gents' outfits and repairs at popular prices.

Welham Road, Streatham, *c.* 1908. Development in this road was mainly undertaken by Swain & Seely between 1904 and the beginning of the First World War, with a few properties added up to 1926. The earlier houses could be rented at 10*s* a week for a two-bedroom, ground-floor maisonette or 11*s* per week for first-floor accommodation.

Salterford Road, off Southcroft Road, in the course of construction, *c.* 1912. The upper reaches of the road were yet to be built on. The houses adjoining Southcroft Road were destroyed in 1944 when a V1 flying bomb crashed and exploded, killing three people and injuring a further forty-three; a newspaperboy out on his early morning round was among the dead.

Penwortham Road, Streatham, *c.* 1912.

Furzedown College and the County Secondary School for Girls in the early 1920s. Furzedown House, dating from 1793, is at the top and the other buildings now form part of Graveney school. Nimrod Road and other roads in this view have yet to have the adjoining allotments converted to housing.

Furzedown House and grounds, *c.* 1925. The grounds once stretched from Furzedown Road in the north to Rectory Lane to the west and Southcroft Road to the south.

The Woodcote Dairy of B. Brown was at 252 Mitcham Road, Tooting. The young man looks rather glum but pushing a well-laden dairy cart around the Tooting streets as often as three times a day wasn't very amusing. At the start of the First World War in August 1914 the dairies in Tooting jointly announced that from that time only two deliveries would be made.

R. Gunner's provisions store at 19d High Street, Tooting, *c.* 1914. The ham joints cost 11*d* per pound and sliced bacon 2*d* per pound. The duck eggs were on offer at 1*d* 3 farthings and chicken eggs were as much as 2*d*. The display of meat in the open would not pass the health inspector's gaze today.

# BRITAIN IN OLD PHOTOGRAPHS

## SUTTON'S PHOTOGRAPHIC HISTORY OF TRANSPORT

To order any of these titles please telephone our distributor, Littlehampton Book Services on 01903 828800
For a catalogue of these and our other titles please ring Emma Leitch on 01453 731114